Shattered Heart: Overcoming Death, Loss, Breakup and Separation

Itayi Garande

Shattered Heart: Overcoming Death, Loss, Breakup and Separation

First published in Great Britain in 2020 by Dean Thompson Publishing

ISBN: 9798611812808

Contents

Preface

Itayi Garande, award-winning author writes, "The death of my father speaks not of death, but of an undying invincible spirit" in his 2019 No.1 Best Seller *Reconditioning: Change your life in one minute*. In this book, *Shattered Heart: Overcoming Death, Loss, Breakup & Separation*, he lives up to that statement as he weaves slender threads of his painful experience of death, loss, breakup and separation into a strong tapestry of responsibility, tenacity, love and personal triumph.

Itayi explains some of the methods he used to overcome pain. Uprooted from his home country of Zimbabwe, facing the pain of separation from family, relatives and friends, he found himself alone in a distant land. His father, brother and a number of relatives and friends died back in Zimbabwe and he went through pain and struggle to come to terms with the loss.

Someone who has gone from that experience to becoming a celebrated businessman, lawyer, bestselling author and a holder of seven academic degrees is someone worth listening to. He knows how to overcome seemingly impossible challenges that many would succumb to.

Itayi discusses emotions that take place when a relationship breaks your heart, a marriage ends in divorce, or when a loved one dies. It will help you develop compassion, providing you with the courage to face other types of losses and challenges, for example losing a beloved pet, losing your assets when you go and live in another country, getting estranged from your family because of your character or simply getting betrayed by people you helped in your life. This empowering book will allow you to develop new ways of thinking and will bring hope and fresh and dynamic insights into your life and your present and future relationships. You will learn how to heal your grief and heal your heart.

This book is a gem and it is full of dramatic narratives. It is focussed on the most challenging human problems.

It has literary merit that is rare in many accounts of personal pain and personal triumph.

I heartily recommend this book.

WILLIAM J. TANENBAUM

Author's Note

A shattered heart is a heart that has been opened—to receive new realities, to be exposed to new pain, but also to receive new love and happiness. When you love someone with all your heart and they end the relationship all of a sudden, you will naturally feel pain and feel betrayed.

This pain is part of life, part of your journey as a human being, but suffering should not be part of your life. It is natural to forget that you have the energy, power and the brains to move on after you lose a loved one, but the truth is that after death, loss, breakup and separation, there is always that ability within you to create a new reality—to move on and create new and better levels of happiness and success.

You can change your thinking after a loss occurs, but you cannot avoid the pain. You should keep moving through it.

My psychology teacher said everyone has the capacity to remember someone who betrayed them with love, not with sadness or regret; but most people choose not to. They choose to be sad and sorrowful and spend time looking for ways to inflict pain and revenge on their exes—wasting valuable time which can be used to find new and lasting love, and create new realities and new experiences.

Even after the most tragic death, the meanest divorce and the worst breakup, it is possible to heal over time. This does not mean that you run away or deny the pain. Instead, the idea is to let yourself experience pain, just like a tree experiences heavy rainfall, thunder and lightning, but a new life unfolds from that experience.

This book, *Shattered Heart: Overcoming Death, Loss, Breakup and Separation* comes at a crossroads in my life. When my father and brothers were alive, I had the liberty to leave all responsibilities to them and just lock myself in my own cocoon. I was criticised for it. I was called irresponsible, reckless and uncaring.

Reflecting back, I am somehow glad that I did that and learned from my mistakes and my experiences. I was the lava that needed physical and emotional protection in that cocoon, only to emerge as a butterfly with colourful multiple reflections. I shimmered and changed—from pain to healing, from an immature boy to a man, from someone who hurt people's feelings and didn't care, to someone hopelessly trying to mend his ways, and from someone who chased money like a lion chasing deer to someone who respects money, life and meaningful relationships.

But, like a butterfly, I am still fragile, but when I stand on my feet, I don't get blown away by the wind easily. I dance in the wind and navigate my way through.

The only difference between a butterfly and myself is that it's transformation from egg to adult was much more graceful. Mine was rough, full of pain, hurt, loss, struggle and deaths of loved ones. I hurt people. I was hurt by people. But during this time, I was growing some new skin under my upper, crusty skin. It was instinctual, not contrived or deliberate. I was slowly shedding off the individualistic, selfish and narcissistic crusty upper skin replacing it with more caring and firm skin—skin that cannot be scratched easily now.

In this book, I express more of what readers of my last book, *Reconditioning: Change your life in one minute* called 'vulnerabilities'. But to me they are not vulnerabilities. I am merely frank about my life and my experiences. I no longer worry much about how I am perceived because it is just that—perception. We are all found in the gutter sometimes, but some of us are in the gutter looking at the stars, as Oscar Wilde said in *Lady Windermere's Fan*. We are all born naked; everything else that we see is drag. No matter what you do, humans will see what they want to see, so you might as well make that transformation for yourself.

The outer world reflects what our inner world is going through. I have learnt that other people's perception of us is a reflection of them; our response to them is an awareness of us.

I know myself better than ever before. This is because my heart has been shattered, but it is being repaired daily. I use the word 'overcoming' in the title of the book because *mending a shattered heart is a process, not an event.* I am clear that my shattered heart will fully mend, but who knows when. The death, loss and separation I face on my journey to a fully-fledged butterfly is, at this juncture, instilling in me a sense of responsibility and a clear sense of direction.

In this book, I hope to impart my experiences to you all who will read it, in the hope that you can also begin to reflect on your life and change it now, this very minute.

You will read about tragic stories—of death, loss, breakup and separation. These stories are meant to inspire and will *never replace professional therapy*. But they are frank—sometimes too frank—to allow you to see that there are people who've gone through painful experiences and emerged victorious on the other end.

You too can do it.

ITAYI GARANDE

www.itayigarande.com
itayi@itayigarande.com

Also by this Author

Reconditioning: Change your life in one minute

The Amazon No. 1 Best Seller, *Reconditioning: Change your life in one minute* is a 'change your life' workbook that will transform your life.

- *Do you want to live a happier, wealthier and purposeful life?*
- *Do you want your life to change now?*
- *Are you finding it difficult to move ahead?*

- *Do you sometimes feel depressed, uninspired and unmotivated?*

If your answer to any one of these questions is 'Yes', then this book is for you. It will show you ways of taking full responsibility for your life and change everything that has been blocking your progress. You will find practical steps to change your life and inspiring stories and quotes to create the life you desire.

It's a *'change your life book'* that is based on real-life examples and stories of how one can lead a happier, richer and fulfilled life. If you understand what conditioned you to think and act in a certain way, you can *break that conditioning* and start reconditioning to live a *happier, healthier and wealthier life.* It is a must-read motivational book!

Excerpt from Chapter 5

In *one minute*, you can *recondition your mind* to think differently about your situation, to break the existing condition that is limiting you. Leaving it to fate will not help. You have to make it happen and you have to do it now. You have to be the alchemist who transforms something common into something special.

PART 1: DEATH AND LOSS

Saying Goodbye to Java

My dog Java taught me to love by giving me his absolute all. I was the centre of his universe. I was the focus of his love, faith and trust. He served me in return for scraps that I gave him and he never complained. Only if we could learn a few things from canines, we would be capable of giving unconditional love and loyalty.

My experience with loss and death started at a very tender age when I mourned the passing of my dog—Java—a Golden Retriever whose fluffy brown hair made him the envy of the whole neighbourhood.

Java entered our large family as a small dog in the winter of 1985 and immediately became an integral part of our lives for what I now view in retrospect as an eventful decade—where my elder siblings grew up and left the family home; and I arrived into teen–hood.

In his later years, Java developed physical problems including cataracts, hard–ness of hearing, crotchetiness, but still had all his teeth intact and was never incontinent.

The friendship between Java and I started off slow. We got Java from my uncle who was a dog-breeder. He was nervous and skittish around people when we got him. His mistrust of everyone was pretty evident because in those days dogs would just be stoned, kicked and beaten up in the neighbourhood for no reason.

But eventually Java warmed up to me, as I brought him treats every day. I was pretty persistent. I would call his name and he started looking forward to it.

He got used to my voice every time I said, "Hey, Java, come and play."

Eventually, he began waiting by the door for me as I came in from school. He looked forward to me coming home with a packet of milk I had saved for him from my primary school ration. We struck that once–in–a–lifetime friendship, but one thing always concerned me. Java slept outside in an open kennel parked outside my door every night. Many nights I heard him sniffing around or occasionally whimpering during rainstorms and during the winter season. I desperately wanted to let him in, but I knew I could not—I was not allowed. A dog was not allowed indoors in my country.

Java died—in the end—from parasite tick fever that invaded his blood. It increased his haemoglobin and platelet levels to lethal levels. At that time, in postcolonial Zimbabwe, there were no vets in the townships and no antibiotics for dogs.

I watched Java gasp a few times before becoming still. I called my father—in tears—and instead of telling him that Java had passed on, all I could do was bawl uncontrollably, tears rolling down my cheeks.

How could I not? Java had given me three years of love. I wanted him to feel safe and loved even in his death.

You see, when Java died, I buried him alone. No one thought a dog was worthy of a decent burial or even a simple burial. I held Java's corpse in my hand. I gave him one last cuddle and placed him softly onto an anthill after wrapping him slowly and carefully in his old, smelly and dirty blanket that I had retrieved from his dilapidated kennel.

I used a stick that I had plucked from a tree to dig up a small, shallow grave for Java. I buried him there and walked away home sobbing. I felt very guilty leaving Java in the middle of a forest. I am, however, eternally grateful that I cradled him in my arms the whole way of bidding farewell to him.

Every morning—for over five years—I sat on the porch where Java most liked to play and sleep on sunny days, in profound sadness and without Java's nose pushing my forearm to rub his back, scratch his ears and welcome the morning sunshine.

Many times in my mind I recalled family episodes starring Java and it struck me that a dog's greatest attribute is to live in the moment, to love unconditionally and to protect. In my saddest recollections, I uncannily found Java standing next to me, pushing my forearm with his nose.

In my head, I recorded many memories. We had no mobile phones at the time and the few photos I had of Java, with his wagging tail, are all lost except for one. My father did not have any fondness for dogs, and he looked hilarious—if not ridiculous—always throwing his thinning hands in the air to keep Java from licking

4

or sniffing them. He never drank beer at my uncle's house, saying there could be dog hair in the cups. I was not angry at my father. Instead, I pitied him for he knew not the unconditional love of a sentient non-human like Java. Perhaps he was just emotionally dry, but who am I to judge.

My childhood friends always remarked on Java's beauty though he wasn't the brightest dog ever. I never took the trouble to train him anything. We were just happy being together, playing and jogging.

Java was perpetually hungry and he would hang around anyone who was holding some food. He loved to run around the yard and the neighbourhood, tail wagging and pink tongue hanging. I spoiled him silly and in retrospect I'm absolutely glad that I did. Otherwise how would I have lived with myself after his death? He had showed me loyalty until the end.

Java, today, reminds me of how the Greek mathematician of ancient times, Pythagoras, believed in reincarnation. Stories are told of how, on several occasions, he would stop and listen to a dog barking, in an attempt to recognise a departed friend.

In high school I loved Russian author Tolstoy's book *War and Peace* because of the section when he followed a dog as he threaded his way through the battlefield after the arrival of Napoleon's troops from Poland into Russia.

Java's death, for me, was not just my first brush with death, loss and separation. It was also a moment when I developed the emotional intelligence to understand the life and its challenges.

I began to understand that life is not just a lumping of years, but of shared moments with family and friends and making meaningful and long–lasting connections; and then it ends, as it must.

Today, and on reflection, I muse that the flesh of humans and animals decays because it is imperfect and after that there is no place for consciousness to reside. It is lost forever.

Java only lives now on an old black and white picture that I have in my briefcase at home. I occasionally revisit the picture to get an emotional glimpse of him, but I never tell anyone. He exists in my heart, but even that memory is perishable. I sometimes spend years without looking at the picture, but I occasionally have dreams of my beloved Java.

My friendship with Java was a rare breed of friendship—in a country where dogs had no place in society, where they were beaten up for simply being dogs. Indeed a dog is a man's best friend.

It is then true that when everything is consumed by time, gone, evaporated and disappeared, all that will ever have mattered is that ineffable, indefinable thing called love. I think of Java today, not as a dog that simply existed in my family, died and was buried, but as a friend that brought me immense pleasure and unconditional love over the years.

Stages of Grief

The seasons teach us many things. I have learnt that just like the seasons change, I cannot be expected to remain the same, but at some point all seasons also come back. So if you think that you have gone through your worst season, be careful, that season is coming back. Just make sure you are more prepared the second, third, or fourth time around.

Psychologists say that the stages of grief for the loss of an animal are just as valid as those of the loss of a human being. This is because death or loss brings intense pain and emptiness in the aftermath. There is no correct way to work through the grieving process. We all walk down different journeys, whether it's a human or a pet that we have lost.

A pet may come to symbolise a sibling, a child, a best friend or a companion that you spend a long time with. My dog Java lived with us for five years—enough time to truly become all of the above and enter and live in my heart. He became part of my daily life and my family life. His death was, therefore, a truly traumatic experience and it created a large void in my heart and in my life—comparable to losing my friends many years later.

I had projected onto Java my thoughts, ideas and emotions: I saw myself in him and the saying that "owners come to look like their pets"—although not a literal truism—was a figure of speech that came close in describing my relationship with Java. He was my self–object.

My kinship with Java was based on the qualities that humans desire in their friends: genuineness, no judgment, trustworthiness, respect, acceptance, forgiveness, dependability, support, thoughtfulness, good listening skills, sharing humour, and love. Java's qualities do not stack up with those of many humans that we know.

At an early age, Java brought me monumental gratitude and happiness. He taught me responsibility, kindness, patience, playfulness, discipline and unconditional love. This was in spite of him eating my food if I left it lying around, scratching me, and eating my socks. Yet I shared my heart with him.

I went through all the stages of grief identified by Elisabeth Kübler-Ross in her book, *On Death & Dying*: denial, anger, bargaining, depression, and acceptance. These steps—referred to as the *Kübler-Ross model*—are not cycled through in a lock-step manner. Sometimes depression comes first, anger second or anger comes third. I will explain these stages and how you can deal with them to overcome the pain of death. These stages are important to understand at the onset because the examples that follow in this book are based on these various stages.

Denial is a part of the grieving process and it is very normal to be in denial about the loss of a loved one. We just don't believe that a loved one is gone and that we will never see them again in our lifetime. It is important to not deny your *grief* when you lose someone and allow yourself to express your feelings in any way that suits you and benefits you. Expressing your feelings is a truly cathartic process that makes a big difference.

Anger is also a normal stage of grieving and it is common people who lose loved ones to become angry, asking themselves questions like, 'Why us?' 'Why me?' and 'How did he/she die?' Was the illness real? Was it a terrible accident? Was it an incurable illness or disease?

Anger at the reason for someone's passing is important because it may lead you to play out your emotions and then start to negotiate and bargain. You start saying things to yourself like: "If only I had not allowed him to go to work that day, he would have lived" or "I wish I had just loved him more because he would not have taken his life" or "I wish I had just stayed at home as I would have nursed her and avoided the death." These constant "if onlys" and "what ifs" can be a source of extreme stress and can be very unsettling.

Depression is sometimes referred to as *sadness* in the Kübler-Ross model. It is important to realise that, for many people, this is the longest stage after the death of a loved one. We will always hold some amount of sadness in our hearts for our departed and loved ones. Time will heal, but there will always be some residual sadness when one dies.

Acceptance is the final stage of grief and accepting the loss of a loved one does not imply that one has forgotten the memories. At this stage, life seems to be getting back to normal and we start doing things that we consider normal in our lives.

We all grieve differently and my late father told me that there are no timelines and no boundaries in the grieving process. You age and personality may determine your level of grief and the circumstances of your loved one's death as well as the relationship that you had with the deceased. For example, people who live alone tend to take longer to grieve because the person that died may have been playing a very important role in their lives.

Try to remember your loved ones by keeping their love alive and remembering the fun times that you had and the moments that you shared. You can keep a framed photo or perform a gesture in their honour; for example planting a tree in the garden in their memory, creating a gravestone that is very symbolic of them or simply retaining a memento from the good times that you shared together.

Keeping these memories of your loved ones can be the healthiest way to deal with the grief of their passing and getting through it.

Soul Needs of the Dying

True friendship is when you do not talk to your friend and you are still comfortable with the silence. You do not think the worst and you overlook your friend's broken fence and just admire the flowers that are blooming in their garden.

A friend of mine, Jasper *(not his real name)* who was dying of a heart disease in South Africa called me on the day that he passed on. I could tell that he wanted to tell me something, but he skirted around the issue. His mother had told me that he was unwell and had no chance of surviving. They had not seen each other in ten years, and his mother could not afford a ticket to go to KwaZulu–Natal from Gwanda in Zimbabwe.

When he called me I could feel that he was afraid of becoming a burden to me, but somehow felt compelled to talk to me.

He talked about how much fun we used to have when we were growing up. I could sense his inner conflict. Jasper had led a fractured life and his strife–ridden family could not offer him much support at this

11

time of need, so he did not want to be a burden to them.

I could feel a sense of denial that he was about to die in his voice, but somehow he found comfort in talking to me—his childhood friend. Maybe that was just his last wish. He had never really been a talker, but I felt that he was entrusting me with his last words and I was not going to let the opportunity slip, so I listened quietly and intently.

The most important thing, for me, was not to push Jasper into talking if he didn't want to. I simply wanted to make sure that he knew I was willing to listen.

He later opened up and bared his dying soul to me. He was raged by the thought of being cheated of life, but was no longer clinging onto the hope that there could be a miracle cure. He was regretful of the fact that he was going to die without seeing his mother. He had last seen her ten years before.

Jasper had what I could call 'soul needs'—the need to be care for, to be heard, to be emotionally safe and emotionally connected. Dying people have feelings, they have needs and they want to be understood, loved and accepted like anyone else. We should always be willing to listen and allow them to die in peace if they entrust their feelings with us.

Jasper died while talking to me.

It was frightening.

The doctor came onto the phone and said, "I'm sorry to inform you that Jasper has now gone into permanent sleep. Would you like me to pass you on to one of our psychologists here at Busamed Gateway Private Hospital?"

I kept quiet.

12

I couldn't talk.

I was coming apart at the seams.

I simply cut off the phone and sat down at a bench in London's Piccadilly Circus, oblivious to the hustle and bustle around me.

On reflection, dying people sometimes have feelings that they have wasted their lives, so they grieve missed opportunities, just like we grieve their death. They may also want to make contact with estranged members of the family, so we should always be open to forgive and forget past arguments, so that we can help them die in peace.

Jasper told me many things that cannot be repeated here, but it is important to realise that dying people may want to confess things that happened in their life, to ask for forgiveness and to die in peace. They may simply want to use a trusted person to convey certain messages to family members, friends or acquaintances they may have wronged in their life. This can be powerful healing for them just before they pass on. My friend died in peace—having told me everything that was in his heart. He was missing people he had not been able to reconcile with in his lifetime.

"Thank you Itayi."

Those were his last words.

Norman Took His Own Life

Some people think that it's holding on that makes one strong; sometimes it's letting go. If you hold on to a piping hot rock you are not doing yourself a favour because sooner or later you will get burnt. But if you release that hot rock from your hand, you let the pain go.

Anyone who has had a friend take their own life will know the painful experience that brings. In high school I struck up a friendship with a teacher who was teaching me technical drawing. I will call him Norman. I left the school after my O levels, but we remained friends for a long–time. Norman was a proud, handsome young man who was very beguiling with women, but he committed suicide three years after coming to the UK.

I never really understood what had happened for him to take his life. I just know how it made me feel. Suicide does not just kill the person who takes his own life; it also *kills the people who love you and leaves an indelible mark in their shattered hearts.*

For me, Norman's suicide eliminated the possibility of life ever getting any better. We all experience challenges in life, but there's always that light at the end of the tunnel. Norman had the chance or opportunity to see that light.

What I know is that when he came to the UK, he had problems getting his immigration papers sorted and he lost two siblings and his father during that time. He couldn't go home as he had no money and his passport was with the Home Office—the United Kingdom's government department responsible for immigration, security and law and order. The painful experience had reduced him to nothing, and he was once again fighting his way through the despair that had devoured too many of his days in what he called *dark Britain*.

The last time I ever spoke to Norman he had told me about his experience in London. I will try and narrate it below.

∞ ∞ ∞

With a grimace, Norman looked around the room where he had lived in squalor for almost three years and pondered, 'This is ridiculous. I have to pick myself up and do something. I am rotting away and am a shame to my family.'

This was his dining room, his lounge, his kitchen and his study. Everything looked and felt painfully familiar. The room itself was a reminder of what he had become—nothing.

'This can't really be happening,' he mused. 'Life has taken a 360 degrees and I'm back to square one.'

He thought of those three letters, G.O.D.

He pulled his feet out of bed and sat on its edge with his head in his hands.

He thought back to the previous three years when he was nothing and entertained the fear that he was indeed going crazy.

He admitted to himself that he believed in God but he had let him down.

If God existed, why were his prayers not being answered?

Why was he in such a mess when he had prayed every morning and tried to live a righteous life?

'Is this the God that I should be praying to?' He wondered.

He let out a deep sigh.

And if God was really here, why hadn't he taken his nightmares away a long time ago. Why had he let his father die while he was away from home?

Sitting in a quandary wasn't helping, so he found his way downstairs, where the situation was not any better. The shared space was just as squalid, depressing and enslaving. The curtains to that dark and dreary room were rarely drawn and spiders' webs had taken over what humans should have looked after and cherished.

Piles of dust had settled on the curtains making them change their original colour.

The penetrating and alluring aroma of the coffee drunk next door made a stark contrast to the squalid conditions under which he and the other house mates lived. The smell of eggs, onion and bacon mixed with something else made its way into this house, interrupting his thoughts.

He retreated to his bedroom wondering what or whether he was going to eat anything that day. He had only just managed to pay the rent that week, thirty-five pounds for the tiny room he called his residence.

As he opened his door, a Bible fell from the shelf where he kept his books, clothes and all his belongings. It was the King James Version which ironically was authorised and included schedules from the Church of England.

'Holy England has done nothing for me,' he wondered as he walked in and scanned the little room once again as if looking for inspiration to live.

But this was a futile attempt to escape from his pain and grief.

Clutching the Bible, he dropped

himself on the bed he had made from a couple of mattresses that had been donated to him by his landlord, Tony Adebayo. Adebayo was a no nonsense landlord who cared less where you got the money to pay for rent, and more about the timing of that payment.

Snuggling like a small child deep inside the heavy down comforter, Norman had only made it through a couple of verses before the Bible slipped from his hands. He had snoozed.

When he woke up, nothing had changed.

The squalor was still very much a reality and Norman decided to step outside into the mid afternoon sun.

He felt an odd mixture of being wrung out like a rag and yet still existing.

What a dreary day this had been and it was barely half over.

For a moment he stood undecided before wondering down to Tower Bridge in the hope of striking a conversation with a stranger, a foreigner, anyone.

British people had shown a disdain and a dislike of foreigners like him. They felt he was one of those people living on benefits and fleecing the system. A year before, he had met an Italian blonde, fell in love with her. She had left him after

her mother succumbed to cervical
cancer and never returned to London.

∞ ∞ ∞

When Norman told me his story, I could relate to it.
Everyone who has settled in a new country has a
story in them—a story of pain, struggle, loss and
heartache.

I have my own story of struggle, of depression, but I
was fortunate to let it play out and come out at the
other end. My friend Norman did not.

I soaked up the pain, the struggle and the challenges
I faced daily. I took in the bad weather and the good
weather because I quickly understood that the storm
would clear and would be over.

Feelings come and go—including feelings of suicide,
giving up and letting all go—but they should not define
who we are and should never define us. There are
many reasons for staying alive. Having thoughts that
are sad and having a continual succession of those
thoughts, does not make one a sad person. We
should always be mindful of our depressive thoughts
and recognise that they can—and will—pass at some
point and we will look back at what appeared like a
problem with shock.

Love and Life Are Temporary

Because of the fact that we are mortal, that we die, that we only live for a while on this earth, everything is temporary. We will leave everything that we have ever worked for when we die. What we see with our eyes is temporary, but what we feel through our heart can never be taken away by another. It is our everlasting and eternal possession.

Talking about the death of a loved one is one of the ways that psychiatrists and psychologists recommend as a way of dealing with pain. However, talking about death is one of the subjects that many people in the West find discomforting and are embarrassed about. Many of us avoid talking about death and this also includes avoiding the people who are experiencing grief after losing a loved one or who are dying.

This subject is very close to my heart because when my brother died back in the 90s, I was greeted with absolute silence when I returned to work. I guess no-one knew what to say to me. In a sense, I felt I was going slightly mad. I thought that after having a life-changing and catastrophic experience, there would be someone at least willing to talk to me about it. I was wrong. Everyone pretended it hadn't happened and I felt that they avoided me, in case I would talk about my situation. I felt like a pariah and could not stay at that job. I left two weeks later, although I had worked there happily for several months as an agency worker.

I find that fear of talking increases our pain. Not only relatives and friends find it difficult to talk about sickness, death and loss. The people who are dying also find it very difficult and very hard to express their feelings and emotions.

Relatives and friends have that fear of making matters worse by saying the wrong thing. They also have a fear of loss. But there is also what is called cure collusion—refusing to come to terms with the truth or refusing to face the truth, or pretending that everything is alright.

People also fear talking to those who are dying because they fear their own mortality, as if talking about death will kill them; or they simply have a sense of shame or guilt about what has happened in the past. They may have ill–treated the person that is dying or were estranged from them, or simply did not maintain good contact with them in their time of good health. To try and connect with them when they are dying might just be too much of a burden to bear.

Others simply cannot face the truth of what is about to happen—that someone they know is about to die.

People who are dying are also unable to talk about their situation. Many things affect their willingness and ability to talk about death and what they are going through.

Life throws us some curveballs all the time, for those who understand baseball. A curveball is a slow or moderately fast throw made with a spin to make it swerve downward. This is usually thrown from the right to the left in baseball. My Canadian friend, Phil, used to say: "When curveballs are thrown at you, make sure that you hit them out of the park."

When you are happy in your life, with no major worries, and with all your siblings and parents alive, it can be easy to think that life will always be like that—that your father and mother will always be there when you need them. You could be fooled to think your sister or your brother will be there forever. You lose sight of how quickly that can end and how fleeting our time is on earth.

Many people find talking about death very frightful, twisted or horrible. I understand why they do not want to dwell on this topic, but sometimes it is good to understand death and pain so that we can remember how truly awesome it is to celebrate life.

We need to understand death and loss to reflect more on how lucky we are to have love and life. These are transient things. They do not last forever. With so much pain and negativity in the world, understanding death and loss helps us notice the love and joy that is often pushed back.

I would be the first one to say that it is not always easy to know how to talk about death, dying and loss. The topic itself brings awkwardness, embarrassment and fear. We worry that by talking about these issues, we are jinxing ourselves, so we tend to shy away from connecting with those who are dying or those who are grieving. But when we do not talk about these topics, we can increase our feelings of isolation, distress and loneliness.

People who live away from home, in the Diaspora have their own experiences of death. This is because when they're uprooted from their communities, they first lose their sense of worth, feel dejected and worthless. These bitter experiences are amplified when they do not have people they can talk to and trust with their bitter experiences.

Unless they can create a new community that can offer support and an ear in times of trouble, the experience can be bitter.

The journey through traumatic grief is a long and especially difficult one—maybe the most difficult life offers. It is also a journey for which there is no preparation.

As mourners, we need the love and understanding of others if we are to heal, so go out there and be part of a community. Do not feel ashamed by your dependence on others right now. Instead, revel in the knowledge that others care about you and are willing to talk to you and listen to your problems.

Digital Rituals of Death

My departed father, brothers and ancestors have one advantage over all of us who are still alive today. These departed souls know that they are still alive and that they will be seeing everyone who is meaningful to them at some time in the future. We mourn their passing, but they are watching over us and rooting for us to do well. We might as well get on with it and start celebrating life.

I was mad at a friend of mine because he had not called me to convey his condolences over the death of my brother. He lived with us in the UK back in the 1990s. He then moved to Australia and finally settled in New Zealand with his wife who is now a respected medical doctor.

I met him in a pub in London when he was a student and struck a friendship that was to last for many years. He had come to London on a government scholarship and the government had stopped looking after him for one reason or the other. That's a story for another day.

I took him into my house and looked after him, offering him employment in my company in all the years that he was a student at London South Bank University. My late brother also offered him work in his company.

On my brother's passing, he sent me a text message from New Zealand—a two-line text.

The text message read, "Sorry about your brother; my condolences my friend! Let me know if you need anything."

I was angry at him for having the cheek to send me two lines when my brother, who had helped him find employment in this country, died. He didn't even mention him by name. I felt betrayed, unappreciated and disrespected.

I later learnt that he was battling lung cancer and the message he had sent me was the last text message he ever sent to anyone. A doctor at the hospital where he was dying had helped him type the message and I guess he didn't give many details because he wanted to keep things private and, besides, he was also dying. His mortality was flashing right in front of him, but he still had the strength to send that final text.

He had read about my brother's passing through social media. I had not even thought about sending him a message, so I was the guilty one in this case. If he was such a good friend, why had I not texted him to let him know of my brother's passing?

In an age of social networking, diaspora communities are actively participating in discussions about death, but there are many issues that this participation brings. Back in our villages, towns and cities, we used to have congregations where people would come together and comfort each other physically, support each other with money and food and their presence.

These rituals are still happening where we come from, but in the diaspora they are becoming less frequent. Unless you were very well known in the community—like my brother was, because he was a businessman and a larger-than-life character—you are pretty much alone when you lose someone. Except for a few phone calls and text messages, you may find that you deal with your grief alone or with strangers that do not know you at all.

Communicating, exchanging information and reconnecting online sometimes gives us the false sense that we are a community and that we can come together when death, loss and separation bring grief. But when the unfortunate happens, you realise that there are very few people who can support you.

Diaspora is an odd concept, especially for people who grew up in two places. You have to balance what you learnt where you come from with the new realities that you face. For example, you have to start communicating your feelings to loved ones who lost someone through text or through social media.

How do you balance these two in a manner that is respectful and acceptable to your community?

In 2018, I had the opportunity to experience three rituals of death—all in memory of my brother. I travelled to Zimbabwe to comfort my mother and we had a funeral there, where hundreds of friends, relatives and community members came to pay their respects. I came back to the UK and there were many people who congregated at my brother's house to pay their last respects to his family and offer their support. Then I had condolences pouring through social media and through text.

This is the new reality and I am glad that diaspora communities are finding ways to navigate the new terrain they are in to be able to comfort each other in times of grief and pain.

Rather than being angry that someone has not been able to pay their respects, I think it is time to try and find new ways of helping each other through the grief. Life in the diaspora has many challenges because we do not have the support system that was there back in our communities. The expectations should be different.

Rather than worry about who or who doesn't pay respects when our loved ones die, we should simply make sure that we start to plan for death before it happens. The problem is that in our communities, death is a taboo subject. We cannot let that continue. Just like life, we should also talk about death openly and prepare for it. It is a fact—we are born, we live and we die. That is not just the truth. It is reality and the sooner we accept it, the better.

Anyone who watched the big send–off that boxing champion Mohammed Ali was accorded will have understood the point that a funeral is not only about interring human remains, but also about giving the dead a dignified burial and send-off. It's also about giving survived loved ones some closure, and a chance to celebrate the life of the deceased. There is nothing sacred about these things, just as there is nothing sacred about talking about death and preparing for it.

A Conversation about Grief

My father's generations subscribed to the popular yet disastrous "push it down" method of grieving or mourning someone's death—ignore it, don't talk about it, and it will go away. I am not of that era anymore. When a child is born we rejoice and when someone gets married we rejoice and celebrate, but when they die we pretend that nothing has happened.

I was recently talking to a friend of mine. He lost five members of his family in a car accident. They were coming from a funeral in Bulawayo. At first I was hesitant to call him from London. I was not sure how the conversation was going to go, but I felt compelled to talk to him and comfort him. My grief had taught me many things that I felt compelled to share with my friend, to try to soothe his own grief.

When you have gone through grief, complicated grief, you learn many things and when people see you later in life, they say, "Oh, you've changed."

"Yes, I have changed. I have been through so many things in my life and it would be ridiculous to remain the same. In fact, it would be impossible to be that person you knew many years ago."

Decades inside a complicated diaspora environment where you are a second-class citizen, where you learn everything on the go, where there is no strong support system and where everyone is concerned about their own survival is not a joke. Even before you lose someone, you are already grieving some form of loss.

When you leave your birthplace, the first thing you lose is your soul, then your family, your friends, your relatives and your community. You lose your nationhood and you become a foreigner.

These experiences cause a lot of grief.

To then lose those people you have left behind is even more heart wrenching, and if you do not share the experience through conversation, you may be headed for a mental breakdown.

Grief has taught me many things. I will try and enumerate and explain them.

The first thing I have learnt from grief is that *I do not have to let grief go, but I have to let it out.* I found my forte—through writing, through my tears and through movement and not just sitting in one place feeling sorry for myself. I have been able to *let out* a lot of stuff that would otherwise cause me a lot of grief. Sometimes when I am alone at home, I have a weird ritual where I lock myself in the bathroom and scream at the top of my lungs. I shout out what I feel and talk loudly to my father and brothers and ask them to give me direction. It is a weird ritual, I agree. But I find that after I have done that, I get clarity that I would otherwise not get. I also get the feeling that if they were in a slumber, I awoke them and they are now watching me and directing me.

Sometimes I just whisper to the wind in the hope that it was not just the wind, but my loved ones telling me that they are around and that they are following me.

The second thing that grief has taught me is that *releasing your emotions is not the same as relinquishing them*. Some people may say I am making myself vulnerable by releasing my emotions to readers of my books. That is true, but I do not expect that to be the end of everything. Releasing for me is not relinquishing my emotions. I am not giving them away. They are still my emotions and my grief is mine forever. When I release my grief into the world by writing about it or through tears, it is free to leave me for a little while, but grief will always welcome itself back into my heart and shatter it once again. That's why we have moments when we cry and moments when we laugh about things our departed loved ones did. It is important to realise this because we should not just support our friends through grief on the day of the funeral. We should always constantly check with them and be willing to lend an ear so that we can help them grieve.

The third thing that grief told me is *what it means to be vulnerable*. We never choose the way we want to be vulnerable. Being vulnerable is an involuntary state of the mind. Life tears every wall that you build without you taking part. It tears apart every label that you give yourself and takes away things that cause you too much pride and bring you back to the basics so that you can understand your purpose in life and your role.

In addition to these three things, I also understand that grief does not proceed in an orderly fashion towards your healing. There are stages of grief, but these do not predict when and how you respond to tragic events and how you grieve. I fell into the trap that grief is forward moving. I was always told that time heals everything, but that has proved untrue. I still think about my father's death of twenty years ago as if it happened yesterday and if grief was forward-moving, I would have been healed by now. It is a long and difficult process and there are constant challenges.

If you have never experienced grief, be prepared for a multitude of different emotions that come in a wave-like fashion. You will also face many situations of grief. Grief does not come in perking order—you may experience the loss of a parent, a child, property and a pet all at the same time. There will be more than one need of mourning, so how do you handle grief in that situation?

Helped by a Stranger

There are people who come in our midst to teach us something and then they leave. I have met quite a few of them. It would be a disaster if you met someone who was supposed to teach you something very valuable and you don't recognise their contribution. Always keep your eyes and ears open. Some strangers in our midst are angels in disguise.

One morning, when I lived in the Tower Bridge area in South London, I went for a walk and I met an old woman. She was throwing stones into the River Thames, with a smile on her face. She looked at me and told me something that rocked my world.

"I can feel your pain," she said gazing intently at me.

"It is very clear and evident all over your face. You need to focus on your life immediately. It is passing by your side. You can't be passive. Make sure that you grab your life by the horns and shape your destiny; you're still a very young man to be depressed or you'll be sorry forever.

"Don't let your grief control your life. You have the power inside you to heal yourself."

I wondered how this woman that I had never met before knew that my dad had passed away a couple of days before. What I was not aware of was that I was emaciating myself by not working through the stages of grief and allowing myself to mourn the death of my father. It seemed that the more I tried to act like I was strong, the more it was evident to everyone else that I wasn't.

After the death of my father, I came to understand that the phrase, "Time is a healer" is simply not true. Time does not heal anything; rather, we heal ourselves over time. We need to find that inner strength to accept that no matter how we could have tried, the death would have happened anyway. We have no control over that. What we have control of is to seek professional help, to allow time for our thoughts and feeling to sort themselves out, and to understand our mortality.

Once we understand these things, we will realise that our emotions and our feelings should not enslave us to a point they control the present moment. In spite of death, there are so many beautiful things, emotions, events that still need to be explored and enjoyed. Death is a fact. Death is reality that cannot be controlled. It would be a shame to miss everything blissful because of something we cannot control. We should never be trapped behind that large and tall wall of grief that we build for ourselves.

One ritual that I perform in order to heal is to always think of the good times that I spent with my late father and brothers. I carry that in my heart all the time and laugh at the jokes they told and the silly things they did. I use the power of visualisation and hope—that eventually I will meet them somewhere when my time comes.

When I use visualisation and imagination, I tell myself that perhaps these three men are looking at me at this very moment, rooting for me to do well, invisible, but present, sometimes shaking their heads in disappointment at the bad things that I do. That makes me fight and soldier on.

Sometimes I 'hear' my late father tell his jokes and I chuckle. I sometimes feel his presence at a time when I am feeling hopeless and almost giving up on something.

He chastises me even in his death and says to me: "What are you doing? Are you crazy? Why are you behaving like a lost cause, not letting yourself enjoy life and succeeding? Why are you blocking all the good things that could come your way?"

Imagine that! Imagine what that does to me. Think about that. When I hear his voice, I lift myself up and face the world. I get up, get ready, show up, with a spring in my step, confident.

If we tell ourselves that we are not alone in the Universe, that our loved ones are not here physically, in flesh, but are here in spirit, how can we ever allow ourselves not to believe that our lives can be amazing? We all thrive and do great things even after having lost so many people in our lives. If death was a hindrance, there would be no progress anywhere in life because death itself is everywhere. Life is offered to us—I believe—as a gift. We all accept gifts, don't we? We must make the best of it, no matter how difficult and hard it can be sometimes. We can. We have the capacity.

Empty Chairs

Remember that people are only guests in your life story, even if they are your parents, your siblings, family, friends or relatives—the same way you are only a guest in theirs. Ultimately the life you live is yours. They will soon leave or you will soon leave them. Make the chapters of your own story worth reading.

Have you ever lost anyone in your life—a parent, a sibling, a wife, a husband, a friend, a relative or an acquaintance? Everyone will face loss of a very close person at one stage in their life. This can be physical loss, separation, breakup or divorce.

There are many religious commemorations around the world. These include Ramadan and Eid by the Muslims. There is Diwali by the Hindus and Hanukkah by the Jews. Aboakyere is a deer-hunting festival by the Effutu people of Ghana. They make a special offer to the god Panche Otu each spring. DÃ¬a de Los Muertos or Day of the Dead is by the Mexicans. They have a meal at the graveyard of their loved ones. Each of these commemorations honours the contributions of those who died or celebrate a past event or a past figure, for example, Diwali celebrates the goddess of prosperity, Lakshmi.

Christians celebrate Christmas and Easter (also called Pascha or Resurrection Sunday)—where they celebrate the birth of Jesus Christ and his death and resurrection, respectively.
These celebrations are meant to help us deal with the pain that we face in losing someone and remind us that we are a society and should congregate and help each other in difficult times.

On one of my family holidays in Turkey, my daughter was gazing intently at an empty chair waiting for Santa Claus to come. She did so with all the anticipation a child could bear. Those who know the story of Santa Claus will know that he got his name from Saint Nicholas, a bishop of the town of Myra, who was known for being especially kind to children. Today, Myra is a town in Antalya, Turkey.
Santa had already left.

We had been late for the presents, but someone had not moved the chairs and boxes next to Santa's chair. We quickly whisked my daughter past the place, but I could not stop thinking how she must have felt, seeing that empty chair.

There's another empty chair that I want to talk about—the empty chair left by separation, by death, by divorce, by separation, by a relationship breakdown, by the journey to the Diaspora.

In my family we started having empty chairs when death entered our world. Instead of family memories sharing special times like Christmas and Easter, I started to remember the lasts: the last time we celebrated dad's birthday, the last Christmas we were all together, the last time we ate together and the last time dad sat in 'that chair'.

In 2018, I went home to comfort my mother over the death of my brother. In typical fashion, I always re–arrange the furniture in the living room when I get home. I think I know it all, so I throw things away which I think my mum does not need or things that 'look old'. I often replace them with new stuff. One day my mum stopped me from moving one chair and she was, in uncharacteristic fashion, quite aggressive about it.

I later learnt that this was the chair my brother used to sit in whenever he visited her.

"Gogo talks to that chair all the time," said my mother's nurse referring to my mother.

"Please don't move it. She also places her bible and hymn book there sometimes."

I sobbed on hearing this.

There was silence in the house and the empty chair was there, staring at me.

Then I remembered a song my dad used to play when we were kids—Don McLean's 'Empty Chairs'. Don went through some rough times in his life after his father died when he was just fifteen. His marriage was on the rocks when he wrote the song and he faced depression. Some lines from the song:

Never thought the words you said were true
Never thought you said just what you meant
Never knew how much I needed you
Never thought you'd leave, until you went

Empty rooms that echo as I climb the stairs
And empty clothes that drape and fall on empty chairs

Anyone who has ever experienced loss of some sort will understand the depth of these words. I was always poking fun at my dad playing old songs like 'Empty Chairs' and Smokey Robinson and The Miracles' 'Tracks of My Tears'—blasé about the deep meaning they carried.

Now with the 20/20 vision that hindsight brings, these hidden gems spellbind me. The empty chairs left in my family every time we lose someone also sadden me.

It is important to remember our loved ones who sit on those chairs that will, at some point, become empty chairs. The agony of separation is real. The pain of withdrawal is unbearable; so do the best you can when you still can, so that you minimise the intense agony that an 'empty chair' brings.

The Ostrich Effect

When we deny and refuse to confront issues that make us uncomfortable, we make our condition worse. Fear should be attacked by action, by acting fast. Burying one's head in the sand, metaphorically speaking, is when you view death as a taboo subject, yet it affects you and defines your reality. You hope that by doing nothing, you will somehow heal. This increases your pain and makes your grief difficult to deal with.

I will end this section on death and loss by discussing how important it is to talk about death. I discussed this in a previous chapter, but it needs revisiting because it is a very important topic.

Many of my friends have stopped talking about death completely. They simply find it too depressing. It is a familiar instinct. As a boy, I would hide behind the sofa in the living room from the terrifying parts of the series 'Hammer House of Horror'.

For someone who has no responsibilities beyond the death of a loved one, there is no great harm in covering your ears during discussions about death.

But when practical solutions are needed in the aftermath of the passing of a loved one, trouble lies ahead if we do not engage and talk about issues that need to be resolved–for example issues related to the management of the deceased's estate, looking after the deceased's minor children and informing authorities about the death.

Behavioural economists have a term for people who actively avoid painful information to try and cope with pain: the 'ostrich effect' meaning people who bury their head in the sand to avoid hearing the bad news.

Of course, real ostriches do not do this and this is the paradox of the phrase—a cartoon notion of what the ostrich is. The claim is that ostrich's bury their heads in the sand when lions are coming and pretend that the danger does not exist.

Two economists Duanne Seppi and George Loewenstein have been publishing many books on this topic, researching stock market behaviour during different times. Their observation was that, online retail investment account owners, behave this way: when the markets are performing well and rising, people tend to log in, admire and marvel at their winnings. When the markets are low and failing, they tended to avoid checking their portfolios to avoid disappointment.

Yet, in investment, bad news is important because it helps you make certain important decisions. Although it is painful, it is useful for decision-making, but the retail investors observed by Seppi and Loewenstein would rather—as real ostriches do not—put their heads in the sand.

In fact ostriches are quite practical and have just been given a bump rap for no reason over the years. They are incredibly skilful at dealing with risk. Although they cannot fly, they have enormous ground running speed, in addition to many risk–avoidance strategies that help them deal with any danger that faces them.

Therein lies the key to which people that face impending death, pain, loss and separation can be better prepared. They should be more like ostriches, rather than being less like them.

They should understand their limitations by asking: "What are my limitations? What are those things, physical, mental or psychological, that prevent me from being better at preparing for pain that is imminent?"

Once we understand what those limitations are, it is time to find ways in which we can better adapt to those limitations. This way, we behave more like ostriches, rather than less.

The challenge is get yourself to pay attention to something that is likely to cause you pain before it actually happens, rather than afterwards.

The "out of sight, out of mind" philosophy is a very easy and tempting one—a short–term remedy for a problem that will exist in your life for a very long time no matter how long you ignore it.

Most of us are slave to, and succumb to, burying our heads in the sand because we desire to escape negative feelings, to protect ourselves from hurt and pain, and because we want to protect our self-esteem. The irony is that when we do not talk about the things that cause us pain—death and loss—we are

already causing ourselves the pain that we are trying
to avoid.

PART 2: BREAKUP AND SEPARATION

Never Judge Anyone

People who destroy you and shatter your heart never render your humanity powerless. You remain human and have capacity to thrive, regardless. Your resilience, your perseverance and your attitude to suffering defines your humanity. The person who tries to render you powerless is the one who loses their humanity. They are weak because they cannot have a relationship with a strong person. Incredible strength comes from not yielding and not breaking. It messes the mind of those who try to control you.

He parked the car and turned to face Maria. He had a look of pure rage and seemed ready to pounce on her. He did. His large fist hit hard the left side of her jaw. Maria's head hit the window on the passenger-side of the car and I heard a loud *crack*.

He wasn't done, though. He pinched her arm and grabbed her hair and then he squeezed her throat.

Somehow Mary managed to croak out, "You loved me once!"

He let go, with disgust on his face.

All this was happening after midnight. She got out of the car that she had bought for him. She was numb, ashamed, and she walked a mile back to her friend's house. He squealed the car tires and raced away from her.

A few days later, she went to Accident and Emergency when she could not move her neck.

"How did you sustain the injury?" the suspecting doctor asked her.

She paused.

"I was at a baby shower party and dancing on the floor with my friends. One of them flung her arm which landed on my neck," she lied.

This was the first of many lies that she would tell about her relationship with Samson. She found it extremely humiliating to talk about her ordeal. Plus, she thought, *it's my fault anyway.*

The doctor looked at the finger imprints around her throat and examined the bruises on Maria's arm. She could feel his suspecting and inquisitive gaze on her as he wrote a prescription for muscle relaxers and painkillers.

"You sprained severely," he told her. "You're lucky that you didn't break your neck."

Later that week, she was in a queue at the British Red Cross offices near London Bridge, waiting to receive some free food. She had no money to buy her own food and her friend had kicked her out because her Nigerian boyfriend, Samson, was becoming abusive and she had refused to break up with him.

Maria's parents had died two years earlier in Zimbabwe and she could not go home because her passport was with immigration authorities in the UK who are called the Home Office. Maria's passport and her Biometric Residence Permit was stamped, "No Recourse to Public Funds". She could not claim benefits or ask the government for assistance through the so-called Universal Credit.

While in the queue for food, a friend of Maria's took her hand and looked her in the eye. "Please don't tell me it's like that, Maria," she said quietly.

Maria looked away.

It did not start like this when Maria met her boyfriend who ran a care home where she worked for a year. Maria had no right to work in the UK. She came on a visitor's visa and when that ran out, she applied for political asylum and *her application got trapped in the immigration system*. At first, Samson was very loving, attentive and sweet, taking Maria out and buying her gifts and bottles of champagne.

She was already in love with him and ready to marry him by the first time he called Maria a worthless piece of garbage in an alcohol-infused anger and fury. Maria was in shock. She thought about leaving him, but she had nowhere to go. She was frozen with indecision. She also loved him. After all she had told him everything about her life, including fine details she had never revealed to anyone. And Maria's mind had started to believe what he said about her: that she was worthless, no-one loved her and that he would get her deported if she ever crossed him. He had told her she was unattractive, stupid, unlovable and incapable of pleasing a man.

The next morning, Samson was sober. He rushed to apologise to Maria, holding her in his arms while she cried. The cycle of abuse began.

The first time Samson kicked Maria, she was walking down the stairs at his office as she had to wait for him at the office until 10 o'clock, and he told her it was her fault. Samson told her that she had "pushed his buttons" and made him furious and angry, so she had to take all the blame. Soon enough, she took all the blame for his rages. Maria was walking on eggshells every moment they were together. He could just snap over something silly and slap her.

Over the course of several years, Maria had been conditioned to believe him when he told her that she would never find anyone better than him and that she was not desirable as a wife. After all, she was uneducated and he had a successful business, so she was lowering his standards.

When she narrated her story to me, Maria said that she thought she knew all about abusive partners and abusive relationships before she found herself in the middle of one. She thought she was experienced, mature and too smart to get involved with someone who would hurt her mentally and physically. She was wrong.

In all her endless discussions with her friend, they had discussed about what to look for in an abusive man. She was sure that it would be obvious and that she would easily walk away if she found herself in such a relationship. Maria had also looked down women who claimed to be in abusive relationships. She had called them weak.

In the end, Maria managed to break the chains and move out. She found shelter in a refuge. Her shattered heart mended, but she was one of the lucky ones. Sometimes there is no time to heal because the abuse ends in death.

Maria did not walk away from Samson and she did not tell her closest friends and family about the abuse—most of them would not have believed her because to them Samson was *a fine man to them*. He was powerful and well liked in the in the community. She knew no one would believe her.

Are Breakups Missed Opportunities?

Loss is an essential part of us. Breaking up with someone is an opportunity to extend your growth and become a stronger person. We have to use our broken and shattered hearts as a catalyst for a better future.

The words that you say to yourself have a huge impact on the words that you utter after a breakup. Would it not be great—after your breakup—to just say goodbye to each other in peace?

You could say, "Thank you, that was a fantastic relationship," and then forget about that person.

Or perhaps you could say, "Thanks. I learnt a lot of lessons from this relationship, take care."

Better still, you could ask, "How was I as a girlfriend?" or "How was I as a boyfriend?"

In real life this never really happens. You are in deep grief and a dark cloud hovers above you when you breakup with someone. The grief is real and can be expected because your heart will be shattered by the end of the relationship. But is the dark cloud supposed to be there? Why can you not be in the afterglow of love instead of being under a dark cloud waiting for a storm to come? Could you find some gratitude somewhere and say, "Wow, that was an interesting relationship, I learnt a lot."

Can you not look at the relationship as just another chapter in your book of life or a scene in a movie about your life?

Many people view being in love as a hill that has no relationship to the valley to which it is related. You cannot have one without the other, so you may as well allow yourself to feel the pain brought by grief after a relationship has broken down.

Constant negative thoughts about being hurt will only add to the suffering that you are currently going through.

Find out from older and wiser people who have overcome the grief that breakups bring. There is healing power in speaking about your ordeal. Do not lock yourself in a room and wallow in pain and sorrow. Meditate, pray; say some affirmations (like, 'I am strong' or 'I cannot be defeated'). These simple techniques, repeated often enough, have tremendous healing power.

Also find some quiet, peaceful time for yourself and to yourself. Silence can have tremendous healing power, but this should not be confused with loneliness. Silence is that profound time you afford yourself to recondition, re-create, reform and grow. This silence—if properly utilised—will help you make a breakthrough after a relationship has broken down. It will help you see the end of a relationship as an opportunity—an opportunity to reconnect with your family and friends, to pursue your dreams, to find a near perfect partner, or simply to gather your thoughts, recondition your mind, body and spirit, and shed off old limiting habits.

The end of a relationship does not necessarily have to be seen in negative light. It can be perceived in good light with the power of positive thinking.

What keeps many people tormented after a breakup is fear. The most underlying fear is abandonment, but also there is fear of being alone, fear of starting afresh, fear of embarrassment, or simply fear of the unknown.

Many people think that they should never break up with the person they are in love with, and that they should live happily ever after. But how do you know that for sure and with certainty? Maybe that's not true. Maybe you were just supposed to know that person for a while, learn some valuable lessons and then go on to conquer the world and be successful. Perhaps you were supposed to understand how relationships work so that when you find the right partner, you know how to grow, nurture and develop your relationship.

What limits many people is the thinking that they should have only one way to respond to a relationship breakdown—the negative way. They go from relationship to relationship and, each time they break up, they are angry and frustrated and harm the person they break up with. They do not see that it is their anger, frustration and desperation that is putting a block on their capacity to form a meaningful and serious relationship with someone. Maybe if they could just change their attitude their relationships would work.

Ultimately, after a break up, you really want to expand your horizon and thinking so that you see many options, opportunities and unlimited ways to deal with painful events in your life.

My own personal experience with relationships, in general, was that they offered me new opportunities to understand who I am. They also offered an opportunity for me to understand my fears and my insecurities, to know where my power comes from, and what the meaning of true love is.

I viewed breakups as learning opportunities, although this thinking may seem counterintuitive because we know that relationships can be challenging, frustrating and heartbreaking.

Whenever I broke up with someone, I was often blamed for being heartless, arrogant, uncaring and self–absorbed. I guess I was, to an extent. But I was learning to love, to deal with people of the opposite sex, to understand my new environment, to understand myself and to deal with my insecurities. There was much more that I was dealing with, rather than just the breakup that had taken place.

Relationships sometimes give us opportunities that we never envisaged when we went into them. This is what the *law of unintended consequences* teaches us. I never intended to be selfish, heartless, arrogant, uncaring and self–absorbed. The intention was always to have a great relationship and be in love. However, other things made that intention impossible. There were *unintended consequences*.

In retrospect, I understand why the people I broke up with thought they were not enough—that they were not complete, that they could not find love, and that they could not create their own happiness in their personal lives. This was because they viewed my actions as selfish and narcissistic.

They did not view my actions as those of a young man who was trying to find his way in life, a man who had insecurities, but who was also at liberty to exercise free will.

They also did not see the breakup as an opportunity to break from a young man who was not ready to love as they expected to be loved. Rather than constantly trying to make me love them more, maybe it was important to be more positive about the breakup and take it as an opportunity to learn new things—about themselves as well as about relationships.

Beware the Jealous Partner

"Jealousy is a disease, love is a healthy condition. The immature mind often mistakes one for the other, or assumes that the greater the love, the greater the jealousy – in fact, they are almost incompatible; one emotion hardly leaves room for the other."
— Robert A. Heinlein, *Stranger in a Strange Land*

For those people who have been in a few relationships, you are already aware that breaking up is not fun and sometimes it can be downright horrible. Almost every break up has its share of drama and tears.

This story is about Ruth, a lady from Zimbabwe who got involved with an abusive Nigerian man. Ruth's story is interesting because she abandoned all of us—her friends and family—when she met Temidayo (or Temi as she affectionately called him) because apparently we were blocking their progress and jealous of their love.   Ruth grew up in a loving family in Harare and her mother was a teacher and her father a professor at the University of Zimbabwe.

She was raised well and was a very loving and trusting friend.

My friend Ruth's journey to hell and back started when Temi moved next door to her apartment in the Docklands area of London. They quickly became friends and later moved in together and became an item. He had her completely and was a real charmer. Temi was also a rebel and for him, life was fast and exciting: parties, dancing, drinking.

Ruth did not see the storm that was coming. They were out one day with his friends and they had been drinking all day. His old girlfriend from Nigeria arrived and she sat on his knee and told everyone that their relationship was still not over and that his real name was not Temi, but Muhammad. She said as a Muslim man, he would never marry an infidel like Ruth.

Ruth shouted at Temi for not doing anything about the incident and for embarrassing her in front of his friends. She left the bar and went to sit in the car, fuming. She was trying to call her friend to explain what had just happened. He followed, bellowing, so she locked the door. He put his large fist through the window on the passenger's side, opened the door, dragged her through it, and punched her in the head.

Temi's friends quickly came to Ruth's rescue and separated her from him.

Temi's friends drove Ruth home. They tended to her sore head, scrapes and bruises on arrival. For Ruth, what hurt more than anything else was that this incident had happened at a time when she had been estranged from her family and friends. Her dreams and her heart had been shattered. She was confused.

The following day Temi arrived at the apartment full of remorse. He promised that he would stop drinking and will never hurt her again, but did not explain the claims made by the woman at the bar, although that was what Ruth really wanted to talk about. She believed him and things improved for a while, although something deep down told her something was wrong.

Ruth later discovered that she was pregnant and he seemed to be excited at the news, but it did not take long before he came home drunk, and after some altercation, he punched her hard in the head, chest and stomach. Ruth ended up at a local hospital with a ruptured cyst in her ovary. The baby was not hurt and returning home, she gave him an ultimatum—either her or his friends. He chose her.

After the birth of their child, the abuse continued and she stayed only because she could not see any way out and there were no options for her with a newly born baby. Things were pleasant on those brief moments when he was sober, and her life became one of moving from one friend's house to another.

She hid her bruises well and he was good at hurting her where it could not be seen. Ruth took several intervention orders on him, which she then dropped after he had either threatened her or promised to stop hurting her.

She was frightened, distraught and knew she had to act to protect her child. She ran away one day and ended up at a Salvation Army refuge—a little scared of the future, but not like she had been for the last few years. The eggshells she had been treading on were gone and she was determined to turn her life around.

A few weeks later, Ruth had a call from Temi. A family member had given him her number. They spoke and he weaved his way back into her life. He convinced her to leave the refuge and they moved in together.

One weekend he went out and came back home drunk, inebriated. They argued and Ruth asked him to leave. He refused. She took her mobile phone and called the police. He hit the phone out of her hand and pushed her to her knees, putting one hand around her throat and squeezing her hard.

She ran outside.

He followed her, pushed her to the ground and started kicking and punching her. She thought he was going to kill her.

A female voice of a neighbour called out, shouting that she had rung the police. Temi fled in panic. If it were not for the neighbour, she would not be here today.

This story is not unique and the same can happen to anyone. I have heard many variations of it and many of them end the same way. Some people are left bruised, battered and struggling to move forward. So how can one make sure that they are not about to become involved with someone who can abuse them?

There are some signs that someone has the potential to be physically abusive: jealousy, isolation, unrealistic expectations, controlling behaviour, hypersensitivity, cruelty to children and animals, striking or breaking objects, use of force during arguments and threats of violence. The more signs of these they have, the more likely they are to be physically abusive. You have to use your own hunch to spot these signs and make some conclusions about whether or not your partner will be physically abusive.

Jealous partners, for example, are very difficult to deal with.

"Jealousy is the jaundice of the soul," according to poet John Dryden and it eats away confidence, ambition and success. People who are competent, confident and with direction are incapable of jealousy in everything they do. Jealousy is a symptom of neurotic insecurity and lack of direction in one's life. At the beginning of a relationship when everything is exciting, an abuser will say that jealousy is a sign of love. Jealousy has no link whatsoever with love. It is simply a sign of possessiveness and insecurity. Jealous people complain about the time you spend with your family, friends or children.

The trouble is that we first make allow jealousy to fester because we think the other person loves us. Once it becomes a habit, then it becomes difficult to deal with in the future.

Ruth was defined by the abusive life she was accustomed to. She was no longer Ruth to her friends and family. The man that was abusing her defined her and it took her a long time to realise that she was not going to get what she was expecting from this man. It was simply too late and she had to be strong if she was to survive and raise her child.

If it is true that heartache makes a person stronger, and that the more hell one endures enables them to fight their way through the treacherous path of life, then there would be no mystery anymore surrounding the heavy weight one feels in their chest. Your heart can be forged of the finest armour by heartache. That armour is what helps Ruth today as she works with abused women in Singapore where she has now moved to.

Fake Friends Destroy Relationships

Fake friends drill holes under your boat and destroy your relationship that could otherwise have been great. They will pretend that they love you, yet they are secretly working overtime on your downfall. It's up to you to know and understand the real reasons why you keep certain people in your life. It's never too late to get rid of dead wood.

I wish I could say men are usually not able to express themselves well when it comes to explaining the reasons why they break up with someone, but I can't. I do not know if I can generalise about all me. I can only talk about my own experience in that regard and the stories I tell may resonate with the experiences of other people.

We are not born knowing how to express ourselves. Our conditioning sometimes does not allow that development to take place. A child that grows in a household where they are not allowed to say certain things or express themselves is likely to be conditioned into not expressing itself even in adult life. That can create relationship problems and can be a source of pain for both that person and the person they end up in a relationship with.

This is why in my previous book, *Reconditioning: Change your life in one minute*, I talk about breaking moulds that constrain us and stop us from progressing. In my relationships, I was not the one to explain anything. I would just end a relationship in a manner that seemed abrupt to the other person, but I would have taken time to look at all options and concluded that the person was better off without me.

This may sound selfish and narcissistic, but in hindsight, the person would later tell me that they couldn't have pictured life with me anyway. Sometimes we were two bitters in a dish and at other times we were running parallel lines that would never meet, so there was really no point in nurturing a dead plant.

In this chapter I want to share a different reason for breakup—the influence of false, nasty and malicious friends. A trusted friend called Michael shared this story. He gave me the permission to tell the story in my own words. He always says to me that relationships are uniquely and personally assigned and there is no point in spending years, months or weeks with a person that is meant to be a passer-by in your life.

This is how he told the story to me and I hope I have done justice to it. This story is about challenges of having a relationship in the Diaspora, is about fake friends, about emotional turmoil and about failure to communicate properly in a relationship.

This is how Michael told me the story:

∞ ∞ ∞

You see, Itayi, I had never been to Elephant and Castle before, so when my friend dropped me off, I plopped down on a curb and checked out my surroundings, scared.

I was worried that from those estates might creep a junkie, a drug dealer, or just a bunch of white boys who would beat the hell out of me.

I stood aloof, catty-corner from another abandoned building that made the slums of Birmingham where my girlfriend, Beauty, came from look like paradise.

I crossed the narrow road, past a man who lay splayed out on his face almost lifeless. He could be dead, I pondered. But I didn't care. I had too much on my mind.

A little pile of objects on the pavement might have been his personal effects, clumsily tied together and looking like something that had been stolen by those who cared for him.

The drowsy luxurious silence of the late afternoon was broken by the sound of a Hummer truck driven by a flat headed man who looked more Ghanaian than Jamaican. I stopped in front of the entrance to one of the estates in that neighbourhood. The estate was notorious for drug dealing.

As soon as it was parked, the motionless, lifeless man stood up and his eyes opened very wide. His eyelids pricked up like a dog's ears. His small red lips opened in a wide jaw-breaking uncovered yawn. You could see the saliva forming in his mouth.

I could not believe that this was the same lump of in-animate meat I had seen just a few minutes before. With his creased face and grey hair, I put his age to seventy-two.

"Good morning," the man said to me, clearing his throat and dabbing at his eyes.

I said nothing back.

My excitement of getting to this place and meeting Beauty was evaporating.

I walked in silence through some very little backstreets where the sun hardly penetrated.

The pavement was so narrow that people who were passing me going in the opposite direction had to shuffle along in a single file.

I came out onto a wider road where there was more hustle and bustle. This made my rotten mood less obvious.

I crossed a pelican onto the sunnier side and I could see my girlfriend Beauty waiting for me with her friend Prisca who I had not seen for a long time.

They were having some sort of tete-a-tete as they usually did.

I suspected they were talking about me, judging from the smirk on Prisca's face when I greeted her. I did not let this worry me as she was a bit of a gossiper and she would act like that all the time.

'Women always talk about their men,' I wondered quietly edging closer to Beauty.

I took a deep breath to steady myself and started talking to Prisca.

"Hello Michael," she said. "I see you're still the hot-looking guy that you were back home."

I just smiled, saying nothing, feeling rather awkward that a friend of a girlfriend would talk to me so blatantly in front of my girlfriend.

"Did I embarrass you?"

"No you didn't." I lied. "You've known me for a long time. Some of these things come naturally."

The smile that had been planted on Prisca's face vanished quickly.

Her face settled back into its usual sullen expression as she tossed her thick multicoloured braids over her shoulder. She always thought I was very vain, but I knew she was the devil, judging from the things she would tell me about my girlfriend, her friend, behind her back.

I was not sure if she liked me or hated me, but I couldn't care less. She was not my girlfriend and I was too absorbed with my challenges in London to worry about her. I liked her though. She was a positive influence on Beauty. She had encouraged her to do more than just have weekends out drinking, but also to have her own career.

Beauty had listened to her advice and she had graduated from university with honours and was beginning to do well in her life.

Beauty's manner was one of quiet composure. She never tried to make false impressions. She was a listener, much more than she was a talker. As an attentive and beautiful listener in an egocentric group of wannabes who were her friends, she could not go wrong.

I also liked her because we had grown up together and she had introduced me to the breathtakingly beautiful Prisca, but who could never hold a boyfriend herself for one reason or another.

Despite her regrettable background and upbringing, Prisca was more than capable of holding her own in whatever situation she found herself. But she had one problem. She could not find a man and she always accompanied her friend to her dates and this was one of those moments—awkward!

We sat at a bar and Beauty went to the bathroom. Prisca could not contain herself.

"Did you hear the news?"

"What news?" I asked.

"Don't tell Beauty please, promise?"

I kept quiet. She continued regardless.

"Her baby father is in town from America. He's come to get the kids and be careful they may be some fireworks in the next few days. You're my friend and I don't want you to get caught up in all the rubbish."

She could tell I was shocked as I never knew that Beauty had children, or that there was about to be a storm. We had been planning life together and I always expressed how beautiful it would be to have kids."

∞ ∞ ∞

Many of you reading this story would know the storm that covered Michael and Beauty's relationship after this revelation. There are two issues here: Prisca's big mouth and Beauty's secrecy.

Michael was visualising life with Beauty and she had destroyed that prospect by holding on to a secret that she had two children. Michael may have loved her with her two children. He, after all, had expressed to her that he loved her and was thinking about starting a family with her.

The other issue is that Prisca knew exactly what she was getting at—destroying her friend's relationship by revealing the most sensitive information with no restraint. Beauty and Michael obviously broke up, but Prisca and Beauty are still the best of friends. "If you choose bad companions, no one will believe that you are anything but bad yourself," says Aesop in *Aesop's Fables*.

Life is very precious. Good friends are not easily found or retained and their actions are important. You should cherish them and show gratitude for them. It is important to show your friend that you care and love for them, and you should do all this as often as possible.

Also remember to be grateful for bad friends and relatives too, as they help you see the value that the good ones bring.

I am grateful for friends that have entered and exited my life because they helped me to appreciate the good ones.

Know Who You Are

Sometimes those things that irritate us about our partners can help us understand ourselves and offer us the opportunity to grow and love better.

My law school friend, Natasha, chuckles every time she talks about her 'dream' relationship that ended in disaster. She learnt some very valuable lessons from that one relationship so much that she is not ashamed to talk about it. She has come to realise her own problems and limitations that made that relationship a disaster.

She is happily married to a man who was not her dream man and she remembers that first 'dream' relationship with humorous delight and the pain is now completely gone.

When Natasha had just completed her law degree at 25 she was excited, overjoyed and full of zest for life after she met George, a structural engineer, at the Students' Union at King's College where her friend was studying nursing.

Natasha was the sort of girl who always hoped that someday she would meet that one special, educated and loving man who would recognise her capacity to love. She always wondered how it could be to be married to a professional man who would complement her fighting spirit and her uncompromising fighting spirit.

After ten months of dating, Natasha felt like she had accomplished her goal of finding a perfect man and had arrived and grown up when George invited her to move in with him.

"It is my destiny to find someone as caring and loving as George," she thought to herself.

"I will work hard and we will have a perfect family and we will be the envy of our relatives and friends. When people try to break us up, I will show them how close and loving we are."

Natasha went from hanging out with us at a local pub in Elephant and Castle, South London, to having high tea with the other engineers' wives in upscale Mayfair and affluent Knightsbridge areas of London. She would take strolls with George in leafy Hyde Park and throw food at ducks in the park's river.

And yet, it was not all perfect. Much of it was pretentious and contrived. George was a bit self–centred and arrogant.

At one point Natasha suggested that George change the way he dress as he always wore oversized, unfitting and cheap suits. She also asked him to redecorate the apartment as it still looked like a bachelor's pad with its one couch, oversized telly and portraits of Rita Ora and Cheryl Cole on the wall and a round bed. He'd had that round bed for many years and loved everything about it and told Natasha that he had imported it from the US as there were no such beds in the UK.

She put changing the apartment out of her mind for the time being, but resolved that she would get the opportunity to change everything at a later stage.

They celebrated their one year dating anniversary with a trip to Ibiza, George's favourite wind down place. Natasha brought two guests with her to Ibiza—fear and insecurity.

She asked George if he had brought other women to Ibiza in the past.

He answered, "Yes, I have been coming here for the past ten years. In fact I met my last girlfriend here."

His honesty made Natasha very insecure.

Let us examine her thinking at this stage. She thought: "Am I just a number to him? If I had not been here, would he have found someone to have a great time with? Am I just a fantasy to him and will he ever marry me?"

Natasha's bottom–line question could be viewed simply as, "Does George love me enough to marry me?"

But it was not. She was so insecure that she was questioning many things, some of which did not exist at all. She had many thoughts: "He is a playboy. This relationship is going nowhere. He can replace me easily."

If you focus on the negative as Natasha did, it can become a self–fulfilling prophecy. You will find every excuse to justify your negative thoughts and, from that point onwards, your relationship goes into decline.

In the meantime, George was picking up negative vibes and negative energy from Natasha. He was beginning to find her annoying, unlovable, unworthy, talkative and moody. So what was there for him to love?

I wish I could say George and Natasha had a great time in Ibiza, but the reality is that she became her insecurities and he became aloof and uninterested in the relationship.

George felt that the trip was stressful because it was their first trip together out of the country and hoped things would normalise on their return to London. However, Natasha's insecurities continued to plague her.

She asked questions like, "Have other women lived here before?" to which George simply responded, "Yes! Does it matter? I've broken up with them."

"I just wanted to find out," she said.

Three days later Natasha asked, "Did you end the relationship or the girls that you dated did?"

With this question, Natasha had moved a notch up, changed her focus from being in a loving relationship, and pushed it to *the end of a loving relationship*. From this point onwards, she was no longer living and enjoying life with her boyfriend. She was already in *grief*. The relationship had gone into decline and was sliding slowly to the end—over thoughts that were merely in her head and of her own making. There was no cheating. There was no infidelity. There was no lack of love. There was just a mindset of one person—Natasha. She has created a storm that was going to consume her relationship and cause her grief.

Natasha's grief and the down slope pull of her neediness, emptiness and insecurity made George realise that there was no longer any need to save the relationship. It was too much of a burden to deal with somebody at this stage in her life. He also realised that trying to reassure her would be pointless and too consuming.

The negative and chilling words that Natasha had been expecting, words that she had pushed George to spit out finally came.

"Natasha, this relationship is not working and I think you should move out right now!"

The negative affirmations that she had had created the situation that she was now in. It was completely of her own making.

Natasha pleaded with him to give their relationship a chance, but he had made his mind and nothing was going to change. She moved out in a frenzy of rage, breaking glass, mirrors and destroying George's clothes and some other personal effects.

She said to him, "I know that I was just a number to you, a piece of property that you can use, abuse and dump. I was always nothing to you."

No rage and destruction she caused helped her. In fact, she found herself in a dark place over the next few days. The insecurities and thoughts that she had brought into the relationship had caused and shaped her grief.

When Natasha told me—her friend she had abandoned—about what had happened with George, we had a brutally frank conversation. She told me she wasn't going to ring him and he would miss her so much that he would call her and beg for forgiveness.

I asked her one simple question: "Look where your thinking has gotten you. Where are *you* in your mind? What is it that would make him miss you?

"When we are together, you're a fun person. Where was your laughter, your great sense of style, your joy and your warm personality? You made yourself boring, monotonous, invisible and then accused George of not paying attention to you. You accused him for seeing you as just another number. Well, now you're probably Crazy Girl Number 6. George is not going to think about *you* and how special you think you are until you do."

What I said finally struck a chord in Natasha. She discovered the negative thinking and negative conditioning that had been limiting her. She realised how ridiculous her behaviour was and how she had failed to put the threads together. Now she would have to deal with her grief, feel it, and sort it out herself.

Natasha finally realised that until she took control of her life, no one else would.
She started thinking about who she was and what her role and purpose in the world was, not in relation to what she considered her destiny as an engineer's wife was, but as herself. Natasha started viewing life as a seed that needed nurturing, not as a vine that was growing on another person's wall. She realised that

focussing on another person kept her distracted from the real work in the relationship—*herself.*

Abandoning Yourself

Many people will abandon you, but always make sure that you do not abandon yourself. That is the ultimate act of self–betrayal. Be kind and considerate to yourself because the signs of pain and struggle will be forever etched in your heart and on your face and they will repel any person that comes into your life.

Abandoning yourself is the ultimate form of self–betrayal. Thinking negative thoughts in a relationship is a form of self–betrayal because from that point onwards you start projecting that negativity to your partner, your children, family and friends.

I have an aunt who was cheated on and betrayed. She never knew, but we all knew what was happening and no–one bothered telling her because she was such a hard–working and positive person, that none of us would dare go to her with a negative story.

I used to visit her when I was a teenager and would spend many hours with her. I began to understand her thinking. One day I gathered the courage to ask her why she was always smiling, happy and full of life.

"Your awesomeness and your positive energy will, in the end, inspire confidence in other people who see you," she responded.

"Wherever you go, no matter what the weather, always make sure that you take your own sunshine to kill the gloom that exists in many people's lives," she added.

"There are people out there who are just mad about something or someone to a point where they don't want to see anyone else happy."

On my uncle's death, I later learnt that my aunt knew all along that she was being cheated on. In fact, they had broken up many years before he died and they lived separate lives under the same roof. I asked her during one of our many telephone calls why she had decided not to remarry and not to let the world know that they were no longer together.

"I realised early on in my life what my true purpose was. I never abandoned myself. I was always in tune with my own rhythm, not your uncle's."

I listened intently.

"I was never going to be happy because of a man in my life. I had my children, my house and my career. That was sufficient for me," she explained.

She added, "So I decided to raise strong men and women and live a happy life with my children. My happiness was not going to be determined by your uncle. He did not have that power and I never allowed him to have it."

"The only person I needed to focus on—the only one I can work on—is the one in the mirror. It's always an *inside* job."

My aunt knew that her actions defined her life and defined how she raised her own children and her health. She didn't want anyone around her to feel the potential pain that she would have felt if she had chosen negativity.

Perhaps more important, she learnt very early in her marriage that she would *never abandon herself*. She found that if she allowed herself to think positive while surrounded by negativity, she was able to attack the pain she felt every time she thought about betrayal by my uncle, meet it with love and understanding, and ultimately heal it. *Her relationship with herself set the tone for every other relationship she had in her life.*

The most important lesson that I learnt from the many conversations with Aunt Sunshine—by the way, that's the nickname I gave her many years later—was that relationships have their own rhythm and their own flow. Once that rhythm or flow is gone, there is not much you can do. You might as well save yourself years of grief and pain by moving on.

Some relationships will last a lifetime. Other relationship will last a few decades, some a few years, and some will last only a few month or even weeks. Regardless of how a relationship lasts, there will always be some pain and some grief associated with the end of it. No matter how long you were with a person, the breakup will bring pain and will require some personal time of grief. You have to learn lessons from it and that gives you the opportunity to understand your own weaknesses, your own prejudices, your own strengths and unhealthy and healthy archetypes.

Some people are shocked when they find out how the repetitive negative affirmations they tell themselves contributed to the end of the relationship and they mend themselves. This is important because it is these insightful moments that bring you closer to real love, healing and mend your shattered heart prepares it for the next bulldozer moment.

Ultimately, the sooner one realises the negative affirmations they constantly play in their head, the sooner they can turn them into positive ones and shape their future life and loves. Just like Aunt Sunshine, they can indeed live happy lives knowing that their true purpose has been realised, than live unhappy lives trying to convince the world that they have a great relationship and a great family.

Uncovering the Gifts in a Relationship

In life, eventually you will realise that there is a purpose and a reason why you meet someone. There are people that will test you, others will use and abuse you, and some will be your mentors and teachers and they will bring the best in you. The people you need in your life are those who truly love you, mentor you, encourage you, motivate you and help you become the best version of yourself. If they do none of this, let them go as they are not useful in your life.

Barbara ran an employment agency for silver service work in London. She met Craig, who was a mental health nurse. She was in her early thirties and he was ten years older than her. She loved the fact that Craig was quirky and had a zest for life. He hoped one day to study medicine since he hated his mental health nursing job. He was only doing it because it offered him a chance to regularise his stay in the United Kingdom as nurses were offered work permits at the time.

Barbara, on the other hand, was a hard-working woman who would work her socks off to get what she wanted and she was a free spirit. She had shimmy skin that seemed to draw the sunshine to her. Craig was a single man who loved life, but did not go out much. He was always at home and she liked that stability—the fact that he had a monthly salary.

However, Craig was dissatisfied with everything, and bored with his life. He was prepared and determined to change his life. In fact, he wanted to find a way into Barbara's life and get out of his.

Craig had begun drinking heavily to brighten his life and have some fun, but she disapproved of his new habit and could not believe that a nurse would not understand the implications of over–drinking. Craig argued that he needed a radical change in his life and there was nothing wrong with some social drinking, so they compromised that everything would be done in moderation.

But Craig hated the idea of a monthly salary. He wanted to be more independent and flexible in his career and with his ambitions. The corporate world was boring for him and he wanted to explore his more creative side and take up photography, firstly as a side hustle and then professionally.

When Craig realised that Barbara was ready to support his career as a photographer with course payments and emotionally, he gave up his nursing job which he said was draining the life out of him, and his salary went too. He wanted to earn a living as a photographer, and although he finished his course and Barbara bought him a photography studio, the clients never came.

"How are you planning on building your business?" asked Barbara some weeks after.

Craig has no definite answer. He just *hoped* that he would get clients and make some money. His studio would somehow thrive on its own. He was also one of those people who thought that material possessions were not important in people's lives and that love alone would conquer all. He didn't see a reason why they should have two cars when they did not have kids.

Barbara started looking after Craig full time and was paying all the bills. Craig also borrowed money from her—15 thousand pounds to market his photography company and buy extra equipment.

When her credit card bill came, that was the last straw for Barbara. Unbeknownst to her, she had been paying for his alcohol addiction and sending money to his parents in South Africa via Western Union. She knew time was up and that this no longer fit her vision of the future.

She confronted him and asked him why he had been keeping secrets from her. He was angry at her and said she had encouraged him to leave his job and start a photography business. Days went by and the arguments got worse.

One day she got home from work to find Craig gone and had taken all the photography equipment and a car she had bought for him. She felt abandoned and betrayed, even though part of her wanted the relationship over. Craig, according to her, had done a bait and switch. She believed that, in a relationship, people needed to grow together and she had trouble understanding how the two had grown apart and how a relationship that had so much promise had broken down.

She felt taken advantage of and used emotionally and financially. In her grief, she directed her anger to herself because she felt like she should have put her foot down from the moment she saw signs that things were going down slope. She also felt that she gave Craig too much latitude because she wanted to support her boyfriend and not interfere with his ambitions.

"What an idiot I was," she told herself and bombarded herself with many other questions.

She paid a lot of attention and gave energy to her mistakes. Her friends had to intervene.

"Stop this, Barbara. You're a smart person, but you're presenting yourself as someone who is inept at life and at relationships."

With the intervention of her friends, she realised that her idea of growing together with your partner was not completely well thought out. In the end, people grow—maybe together, but also maybe alone. As an optimistic, full of life person, she was deluded to think that growth always meant growing with your partner, rather than *helping each other grow towards some goal today and in the future.*

Barbara was finally able to see that her relationships were controlled and ruled by fear. Fear that, although she was a successful businesswoman, she would end up alone, and fear that Craig would leave her.

There was no intersection in their lives—no growing together, only pulling apart. It was clear from the start that the relationship was never going to last because Barbara admired aspects of Craig's life, that Craig himself hated. Their personal destinies clashed.

Relationships are meant to move towards some higher good and love, not fear, should guide them. If these two are missing, there may be nothing to stay for anymore. You can fool yourself as much as you want that you are happy, but you are living in fear if there is no higher good to reach. You are starving yourself an opportunity to be truly happy by staying with someone out of fear.

Do not focus only on the person you are attracted to. Also, focus on yourself and try to find out if you are coordinated on your ambitions. If there is nothing in sync, do not hold on because family, friends or society expects you to be in a relationship. You *always have a choice*: you can continue to fool yourself that you are in love, when you're simply fearful or you can release them with love.

You Are On Your Own After Divorce

I was never divorced myself, but I have vicariously experienced divorce through my work and through experiences of family members and friends. It is painful, but it isn't such a tragedy. The tragedy for me was for my loved ones to stay in an unhappy marriage, teaching their children the wrong things about marriage and love. I'm yet to see someone die of a disease called divorce.

When did you know it was over? I asked a friend after she had gone through a very expensive, nasty and emotionally draining divorce. This is a very common question that people ask divorcees. Tracy told me that she knew it was all over when she could look at her children in the eye and tell them that it was over and when the children asked why they had divorced.

Tracy had been previously convinced that she could make the marriage work. She had tried her best. She had cried, pleaded, begged, threatened, but got nothing. Nothing she did could change the impasse, the bitterness and the resentment.

When Tracy's husband finally moved out, she reported of a strange, peaceful and serene environment in her house; but she also felt slightly panicky and terrified, realising that she was now on her own. Everything from that point onwards was to be decided and done by her and no one else.

She didn't have any regrets—none about her marriage and none about her decision to divorce because she would have lost her mind, her dignity, her integrity and possibly her life if she had remained in that marriage. Her husband of fifteen years never forgave her for making the final plunge. He wanted to make the decision, so she beat him to it and he was angry because of that—not because of the reasons for the divorce.

Tracy's husband told his children that their mother destroyed the family, but to her, the divorce saved the family and saved her. Staying together was more toxic than staying apart. Tracy puts it this way: "It is better for children to come from a broken home than to grow up in a broken home."

Grief is indeed 'the emotional contract of divorce' as writer Cheryl Nielsen said, but it should never stop one from moving on after a bitter divorce. There will definitely be times that one will experience sadness, happiness, anger and other mixed emotions after a nasty divorce or separation, but in the end, it will be for the person's good.

Marriage should be enjoyed and not endured. It is not a sport that needs endurance. This is real life and you have one shot at it. So why mess your one shot at life by staying in an unhappy, unhealthy and toxic marriage?

Play Your Side of the Relationship

Many people in the world are lonely, not because they are abandoned by friends, but because they build walls around themselves instead of bridges. Even when they build bridges, they fail to realise that bridges have no allegiance to either side.

We have read about many examples of relationship problems and challenges. There is a lot we can all do to limit the grief that breakup and separation causes. Think of your situation as a game of tennis that you are playing with someone else. You cannot control the other side. You only control your own thoughts, intentions and actions—not the thoughts of the player on the other side.

One of the biggest mistakes that grieving people do is to try and control what the other side is doing. They strategise and try to control and operate what the other person is doing. This is not just impossible, but also counterproductive. It will not work and it attracts resistance from the other party.

In a game of tennis, you can strategise as much as possible, but you will never be able to understand what the other player is planning until they have already executed their plan.

Focus on what you are doing and help yourself heal, and that starts with changing your mindset and the way you think. *It starts by reconditioning your mind.* You don't recondition your mind to convince the other person that they should be with you, but to be able to deal with the grief that comes with loss, separation and breakup.

In a game of tennis, one way of doing this is to convince yourself that you are a serious player who can win the match and concentrate of the prize winning the match. That is the only goal that you have to achieve in this game. Have positive thoughts that you are indeed a real player, a skilful and experienced one. Do not let the other player control your mindset.

Pay attention to your thoughts and your thought process.

Are your thoughts limiting you?

Are you blaming the other person as a way of dealing with your grief?

Listen carefully to the voice within because that is the voice that you are battling. It is not the person you are breaking up with. That person is already gone and there's nothing you can do about it. The person is gone for a reason. The reason is that this was a bad relationship and there was no reason for saving it. If this is the case, why then would you want to save it? You think you need the relationship, but you don't.

Think of your thoughts as energy. What kind of energy are you bringing to yourself and what are you settling for? Who is pushing that energy to you? Do you need that energy or not. When breakup or separation happens, you could take the easier route of getting angry with the other person, but that does nothing for you in the end.

When a relationship ends, do not obsess about the other person. You are just wasting your time by asking questions and making statements like:

Is she thinking about me?

I have to prove myself and win her back?

I will dress well to attract him back.

He will see what he is missing.

Is he happy with his new girl?

People who live in the past cook up all these questions and statements. That probably did not take place in the way that you see it anyway. Maybe he or she never really loved you, so how can you win them back?

Try to bring your energy and your thoughts to the present. This is what matters, not your perception of the past. The past is gone and the ball is on the other side of the court.

Come back to your side of the tennis court.

Who is managing *your* life if all your thoughts are about how to manipulate and control the other person?

Who is taking care of *you*, sorting out your grief and making sure your insecurities are dealt with?

You want your ex was to love and care for you. How can they do that when they are gone and when you are incapable of loving yourself?

Mending a Shattered Heart

Mending anything starts by thinking about possibilities and change is a process of our thinking. People who do not change their thinking cannot mend a shattered heart. It is people who adjust their thinking that can mend a shattered heart. The rest shatter with their shattered heart.

It is not death, loss, separation or breakup that worries us. It's the questions we ask ourselves when we think about these things:

Will there be pain?

What will it feel like?

We are not asking how it will be like to be dead or to be separated from loved ones. It's interesting that when faced with trouble, people say, 'I wish I was dead' or 'I wish I was not in this relationship'. But no one wants to actually go through with that wish. This is not because they know how it feels to be dead. It's because they worry about *how* they are going to die,

93

how their children will live without them, *how* others will feel when they are gone.

This is our conditioning. We are made to think of death as a very painful process, so we find it very difficult to imagine how our loved ones felt when they were dying. But maybe they are more peaceful now. Maybe they never want to come back to this place and face the problems they were facing when they were alive in flesh.

When we break this conditioning and remove some of the fear around dying, we need to replace them with something that allows a good death, a reasonably good separation and breakup.

The best way is to start preparing for our death. When you have money or resources reserved for your death, you know that your loved ones will not suffer in the event that you die today. They will also be comfortable knowing that everything is in place in case death comes suddenly. This way, we begin to break the conditioning and start moving forward. This will not get rid of the grief that follows death, but it will reduce the pain associated with death.

We, as human beings, are all psychologically equipped to deal with death, loss, separation and breakup. We cannot stop them from happening—but we can control our actions, our thoughts, and our attitude to them.

Grief has to do with the heart and soul. Allow yourself time to mourn and grieve, so that your heart and soul can mend. Suffering, for me, is what is optional because once you adjust your thinking; you can eliminate your pain. You can start by reconditioning your mind to think positive, treating others with compassion, and then replace sorrow with hope. You can choose your words wisely and make sure that you are kind to yourself. Pay a lot of attention to how you think and strive daily to make changes to your thoughts, especially negative thoughts that rob you of your peace. This will help you bring more happiness in your life and transform it. Do not try too much to change the other person.

Change yourself.

The End